Samuel French Acting Edition

CW00481667

Southern Pi
A Slave's Road to Freedom

Inspired by
The Great Escapes: Four Slave Narratives

by Thomas Bradshaw

SAMUELFRENCH.COM   **SAMUELFRENCH.CO.UK**

FOR PRODUCTION ENQUIRIES

UNITED STATES AND CANADA
Info@SamuelFrench.com
1-866-598-8449

UNITED KINGDOM AND EUROPE
Plays@SamuelFrench.co.uk
020-7255-4302

Each title is subject to availability from Samuel French, depending
upon country of performance. Please be aware that *SOUTHERN
PROMISES* may not be licensed by Samuel French in your territory.
Professional and amateur producers should contact the nearest Samuel
French office or licensing partner to verify availability.

For all enquiries regarding motion picture, television, and other media rights, please contact Samuel French.

MUSIC USE NOTE

Licensees are solely responsible for obtaining formal written permission from copyright owners to use copyrighted music in the performance of this play and are strongly cautioned to do so. If no such permission is obtained by the licensee, then the licensee must use only original music that the licensee owns and controls. Licensees are solely responsible and liable for all music clearances and shall indemnify the copyright owners of the play(s) and their licensing agent, Samuel French, against any costs, expenses, losses and liabilities arising from the use of music by licensees. Please contact the appropriate music licensing authority in your territory for the rights to any incidental music.

IMPORTANT BILLING AND CREDIT REQUIREMENTS

If you have obtained performance rights to this title, please refer to your licensing agreement for important billing and credit requirements.

SOUTHERN PROMISES premiered at Performance Space 122 in New York City on September 7, 2008. The performance was directed by José Zayas, with set design by Ryan Elliot Kravetz, lighting design by Evan Purcell, sound design by David M. Lawson, and costume design by Carla Bellisio. The production stage manager was Teddy Nicholas. The cast was as follows:

ISAIAH	Peter McCabe
ELIZABETH	Lia Aprile
DAVID	Jeff Biehl
JOHN	Hugh Sinclair
BENJAMIN	Erwin E. A. Thomas
CHARLOTTE	Sadrina Johnson
PETER / IMAGINARY SLAVE	Derrick LeMont Sanders
DOCTOR / CLERK / MAN 2	Matt Huffman

SOUTHERN PROMISES was presented in conjunction with the Immediate Theatre Company and Queens Theatre in the Park as part of B.O.B., P.S. 122's interborough commissioning program. Produced in collaboration with the David Schwartz Foundation.

SOUTHERN PROMISES was produced at the Flea Theater in New York City from March 11–April 18, 2019. The production was directed by Niegel Smith, with scenic design by Jason Sherwood, lighting design by Jorge Arroyo, sound design by Fabian Obispo, and costume design by Claudia Brown. The production stage manager was Anna Kovacs. The cast was as follows:

ISAIAH	Darby Davis
ELIZABETH	Brittany Zaken
DAVID	Jahsiah Rivera
JOHN	Marcus Jones
BENJAMIN	Shakur Tolliver
CHARLOTTE	Yvonne Jessica Pruitt
ATTICUS	Adam Coy
IMAGINARY SLAVE / EMMANUEL	Adrain Washington
DOCTOR	Timothy Park
SARAH	Selamawit Worku

SOUTHERN PROMISES was developed, in part, through IRT Theater's Artist in Residence Program. www.irttheater.org. Production Assistance Grant provided by New York Theatre Workshop.

CHARACTERS

ISAIAH – (32) the master of the plantation

ELIZABETH – (28) his wife

DAVID – (30) Isaiah's brother

JOHN – (32) Elizabeth's brother, a minister

BENJAMIN – (32) a loyal slave

CHARLOTTE – (30) Benjamin's wife, a light-skinned mulatto slave; she should look almost white

ATTICUS

IMAGINARY SLAVE

DOCTOR

SARAH

EMMANUEL

SETTING

Louisa County, Virginia, forty-five miles from the city of Richmond. The play takes place on a small plantation.

TIME

The year is 1848.

AUTHOR'S NOTES

This play includes excerpts from firsthand accounts written by former slaves, including Daphne Brooks, William Wells Brown, Henry Box Brown, and William Craft, whose stories are collected in *The Great Escapes: Four Slave Narratives*. These accounts were approximately written between 1848 and 1860.

The Prologue is only to be used if the play is being performed entirely by people of color. If the show is being performed by POC, then the characters of Benjamin and Charlotte should be played by actors from the African diaspora. The rest of the cast can be made up of anyone who does not identify as white. It's fine if they look white, as long as they don't identify as being solely Caucasian. If the play is being cast traditionally, i.e. white people as slave owners and black people as slaves, just start with Scene One.

For the production at the Flea Theater, the Prologue was incorporated into the pre-show speech that is given before each show. Different actors read sections of the monologue for the Flea production, but it would be fine for one actor to read the entire thing. The Prologue on the next page is the text on its own.

Prologue

We would like to say a word about why we've decided to present Thomas's play, *Southern Promises*, the way we have – specifically, only casting people of color, us, in this production. Many cultures and religions retell and relive traumatic events from their histories as a way to honor those who suffered, and as a method of healing and ensuring that the past does not repeat itself.

People of color in America don't really have a tradition where we confront and investigate the legacy of slavery on our own terms. This legacy is the root of all societal racism in this country, and we as a society are just starting to dig our way out. That's why we've decided to put on this play tonight. We hope you enjoy and are moved by what we've put together for you.

Oh, and one more thing. I've always thought of myself as a black person, the descendant of slaves. That's true, but it turns out I'm just as white as I am black. You see, I took a DNA test last month. The results say that I'm forty-eight percent European, forty-nine percent Sub-Saharan African, and three percent other things including Native American, Filipino, and South Asian! Anyway, the point is that I'm almost half white, even though you wouldn't know that by looking at me.

My mother always told me my white blood was rape blood. But what am I supposed to do with that information? Am I supposed to reject fifty percent of who I am? Pretend that it doesn't exist? Look down upon it? Feel shame about it? I can't change the past, and I can't reject an essential part of who I am. The only path forward for me is to fully embrace the entirety of my lineage.

My ancestors threw tea into Boston Harbor. My ancestors served in the court of Henry VIII. My ancestors pillaged the diamond mines of South Africa. They also overthrew the white imperialists in Haiti, and beat drums and danced during the Congolese sunset. All of this is me, and I embrace it all.

This means that I'm just as much slave owner, as I am slave. Both the oppressor and the oppressed. This contradiction is an essential part of who I am, and I choose to embrace it all. Every character in this show is me. Every one of these characters are my ancestors.

Scene One

(At rise are **ISAIAH** *and* **ELIZABETH**. **ISAIAH** *is on his deathbed. He has rheumatism and tuberculosis. He is in the midst of a coughing fit.)*

ELIZABETH. *(Strokes his head.)* How are you feeling dear?

ISAIAH. The rheumatism seems better, but I can't manage this cough. Beth, I'm scared.

ELIZABETH. About what?

ISAIAH. I think I'm going to die tonight.

ELIZABETH. Hush your mouth. You are not going to die under my watch, Isaiah. You're a good man and you've led a good Christian life, therefore you have nothing to fear. God will heal you and sustain you.

ISAIAH. Even the holiest of men must eventually die.

ELIZABETH. You quit this morbid talk. You hear me?

ISAIAH. *(Has another violent coughing fit.)* I had my lawyer change my will last week.

ELIZABETH. What do you mean?

ISAIAH. I'm going to free all of our slaves after I die.

ELIZABETH. Your fever must be rising. I'm going to call the doctor.

> *(She starts to leave the room, but he grabs her arm.)*

ISAIAH. Listen to me Beth. I have had a lot of time to ponder this since I've been bedridden, and I've come to the conclusion that the abolitionists are right. I have come to believe that slavery is a mortal sin and a blight upon our civilization. In order to cross the gates of heaven my slaves must be emancipated.

(ELIZABETH is silent.)

ISAIAH. I know this is hard for you to hear, but trust me Beth. It is god's will.

(He has another coughing fit.)

Will you promise me that you will see to it that our slaves are freed upon my death?

(Long pause.)

ELIZABETH. I promise.

(They kiss.)

ISAIAH. You have given me the best years of my life. I love you.

ELIZABETH. I love you too.

ISAIAH. Will you fetch Benjamin?

ELIZABETH. Of course.

(She starts to leave.)

ISAIAH. And fetch Isaiah Junior too. I want him to witness what a good man I am, so that he can carry on our family's legacy.

*(**ELIZABETH** nods her head and leaves the room.)*

*(She returns with **BENJAMIN** and her infant son, **ISAIAH**. She holds him in her arms.)*

BENJAMIN. You wanted to see me massa?

ISAIAH. Come close Ben.

*(**BENJAMIN** goes to **ISAIAH**'s bedside. **ISAIAH** has another coughing fit.)*

BENJAMIN. Do you want me to fetch you some water?

ISAIAH. No. Just hold my hand and stay with me.

*(**BENJAMIN** takes **ISAIAH**'s hand.)*

How's your wife?

BENJAMIN. Charlotte's well massa. She's awful sad about your illness. All the slaves is sad. You's the kindest massa a slave could ever hope for.

ISAIAH. Do you remember when we were children Ben? How we used to catch June bugs by that creek at the edge of the plantation.

BENJAMIN. I sure do massa. Those was some good times.

ISAIAH. *(Starts to laugh.)* And how we used to scare my sister Mary half to death by jumping out of the bushes when she'd be walking up the road from town.

> *(They both laugh.)*

You know Ben, I've always thought of you as a brother. I want you to know that.

BENJAMIN. I'm honored massa. I've always loved you.

> *(ISAIAH kisses BENJAMIN's hand.)*

ISAIAH. I've decided to emancipate you after I die.

BENJAMIN. What? What do you mean by emancipate?

ISAIAH. It means that you're going to be free Benjamin. You, your wife, and all my other slaves – free.

BENJAMIN. I don't know what to say massa. Thank you! Thank you! You's a saint. Gabriel and Saint Peter will welcome you at the gates of heaven.

ELIZABETH. I think your master needs to be left alone now to get his rest Benjamin.

BENJAMIN. Yes, of course missus.

> *(He starts to leave, but ELIZABETH stops him at the door.)*

ELIZABETH. Benjamin, I don't want you to repeat what the master told you just yet. I don't want the other niggers to get too excited. After all, with god's help the master might live another few years.

BENJAMIN. Yes ma'am.

> *(He exits.)*

Scene Two

(At rise, we hear funeral bells. Word has just gotten out on the plantation that Isaiah is dead. Benjamin's wife, **CHARLOTTE**, *is weeping alone onstage.* **BENJAMIN** *enters and says nothing at first.)*

BENJAMIN. I guess you heard that massa's dead.

CHARLOTTE. *(Softly.)* Yes. He was a good man.
He treated us so well. What will become of us now?

BENJAMIN. What do you mean?

CHARLOTTE. Suppose mistress sells us? We may never see each other again. Suppose we get bought by a cruel massa who whips us for every little thing. Aren't you afraid?

BENJAMIN. I have to tell you something.

CHARLOTTE. What?

BENJAMIN. You have to swear to secrecy.

CHARLOTTE. I swear.

BENJAMIN. I'm just as sad as you are that massa's dead. You know he was like a brother to me. But while he was on his deathbed, god bless his soul, he told me that we was gonna be free after he died.

CHARLOTTE. Free?

BENJAMIN. Yes. He said that we was gonna be free. It's in his will.

CHARLOTTE. *(Drops to her knees.)* Hallelujah! Praise the good lord!
Do you know what this means Benjamin? It means that we can start a family.

BENJAMIN. *(Overjoyed.)* I know!

CHARLOTTE. I always wanted to have a baby with you, but I ain't wanted to bring no baby into this world if it gonna be born a slave. I'd rather kill my own child than have it grow up in bondage.
Now we can have a baby that'll be born free! Hallelujah!

(They start to kiss and take off each other's clothes, and then **CHARLOTTE** *stops suddenly.)*

Are you sure?

BENJAMIN. Sure about what?

CHARLOTTE. That we're gonna be free.

BENJAMIN. Yes. Don't worry. Now lay back so that we can start a family.

(They giggle.)

*(***CHARLOTTE*** lays back and ***BENJAMIN*** enters her. They have sex as the lights fade to black.)*

Scene Three

*(At rise, **ELIZABETH** is onstage alone. **BENJAMIN** enters.)*

BENJAMIN. You wanted to see me ma'am?

ELIZABETH. Yes Benjamin, I have an urgent matter that I must discuss with you.

BENJAMIN. What is it?

ELIZABETH. You haven't told any of the slaves about the conversation that you and your master had on his deathbed, have you?

BENJAMIN. No ma'am.

ELIZABETH. Your master had a high fever and was delirious when he told you that you would be free. You will not be freed. It is god's will that you remain on this plantation until your dying day. Do you understand?

BENJAMIN. *(Hesitant. Heartbroken.)* Yes ma'am.

ELIZABETH. Good. Now take off your shirt.

BENJAMIN. Why ma'am?

ELIZABETH. Your place is not to ask me questions. Take off your shirt nigger.

> *(**BENJAMIN** takes off his shirt.)*

Now take off your pants.

> *(He hesitates and takes off his pants. He is completely naked.)*

Very good Benjamin.

Now lift up my dress and climb on top of me.

BENJAMIN. *(Very hesitant. Almost crying.)* But ma'am. My wife.

ELIZABETH. If you don't do as I say I'll have you whipped until your blood runs like a river! Now lift up my dress and climb on top of me nigger!

> *(He lifts up her dress and climbs on top of her.)*

You know what to do Benjamin.

(He enters her and she lets out a moan. He starts to move back and forth inside her.)

Faster nigger! Faster!

(He's pounding into her as hard as he can, and she has an orgasm. He has an orgasm a few moments later.)

(They are still. **BENJAMIN** *is guilt-ridden.)*

Now go fetch me some coal. The furnace in the kitchen is running low.

*(***BENJAMIN*** *pulls out of her and gets out of the bed.* **ELIZABETH** *puts her dress back over her legs.* **BENJAMIN** *puts back on his clothes.* **ELIZABETH** *sits up and watches him leave.)*

Scene Four

(At rise, **ELIZABETH** *and her brother-in-law,*
DAVID, *are in the parlor of her house.)*

DAVID. How are you holding up Beth?

ELIZABETH. It's very difficult to manage now that your brother Isaiah is gone. I miss him so much.

DAVID. We must find comfort in the fact that he's at home with Jesus now.

ELIZABETH. That is a comfort. But he was so young. Our son probably won't even remember him when he grows up.

DAVID. God works in mysterious ways. We must not question god's will.

ELIZABETH. Yes.

DAVID. How is my nephew?

ELIZABETH. He's very healthy. I thank god for that.

DAVID. Isaiah's spirit lives on in him.

ELIZABETH. Indeed.

DAVID. So Elizabeth, how are you going to go about setting your slaves free?

ELIZABETH. What?

DAVID. Isaiah told me that he willed his slaves to be set free after he died.

ELIZABETH. I was not aware that Isaiah had corresponded with you about that matter.

DAVID. Indeed he did. He asked me to see to it that his wishes were executed properly.

ELIZABETH. I have no patience with people who set niggers at liberty. It is the very worst thing you can do for them. It is true that my dear husband just before he died willed his niggers free. But I and all our friends know very well that he was too good a man to have ever thought of doing such an unkind and foolish thing, had he been in his right mind. Therefore I had the will altered as it should have been in the first place.

DAVID. Do you mean, Beth, that willing the slaves free was unjust to yourself, or unkind to them?

ELIZABETH. I mean that it was decidedly unkind to the servants themselves. It always seems to me such a cruel thing to turn niggers loose to fend for themselves, when there are so many good masters to take care of them.

I care nothing for the niggers, on my own account, for they are a great deal more trouble than they are worth, I sometimes wish that there was not one of them in the world, for the ungrateful wretches are always running away.

DAVID. If they are so much trouble, then why not set them free and release yourself from the burden of caring for them?

ELIZABETH. There is no good reason why property should be squandered! If my son and myself had the money for those valuable niggers, just see what a great deal of good we could do for the poor, and in sending missionaries abroad to the poor heathen, who have never heard the name of our blessed redeemer. My dear brother who is a Christian minister has advised me to sell every blessed one of them for what they will fetch, and go live in peace with him in New York.

DAVID. Your brother being a good Christian minister, it's strange he did not advise you to let the poor negroes have their liberty and go north.

ELIZABETH. It's not at all strange David, it's not at all strange. My brother knows what's best for niggers; he has always told me that southern niggers were much better off than the free niggers in the north. In fact, I don't believe there are any white laboring people in the world who are as well-off as the slaves.

DAVID. You are quite mistaken Beth. For instance, my great aunt before she died, emancipated all her slaves, and sent them to Ohio, where they are getting along well. I saw several of them last summer myself.

ELIZABETH. Well, freedom may do for your aunt's niggers, but it will never do for mine; and plague them, they shall never have it!

DAVID. What about Benjamin, won't you at least free him? Isaiah and I grew up with Benjamin and feel a strong bond towards him.

ELIZABETH. I will not free Benjamin, but I won't sell him either. I plan to bring him to New York to serve me.

DAVID. I see that I can not change your mind, so I will take my leave of you. It was lovely to see you Beth.

ELIZABETH. It was a pleasure to see you David. Take care of yourself.

(**DAVID** *exits.*)

Scene Five

(At rise, it is three weeks later. **DAVID,** *and Elizabeth's brother,* **JOHN,** *have shown up unannounced. They knock.* **BENJAMIN** *answers the door.)*

BENJAMIN. Hello Master David, hello Reverend John. Do you want to see the mistress?

DAVID. Yes Benjamin, may we come in?

BENJAMIN. Of course. You can wait in the parlor, and I'll fetch her.

JOHN. Thank you Benjamin.

*(***BENJAMIN*** shows them to the parlor, then goes to find Elizabeth.* **ELIZABETH** *enters a few moments later.)*

ELIZABETH. What on earth are you two doing here? John, why aren't you in New York?

JOHN. As your brother, it is my sacred duty to make sure your affairs are in order after such a tragic event. I'm so sorry that I couldn't be here for Isaiah's funeral.

ELIZABETH. What matters is that you're here now. I'm so happy to see you!

(They embrace.)

JOHN. There's an urgent matter that we wish to speak to you about.

ELIZABETH. Nothing's wrong I hope!

JOHN. No. No. Quite the opposite.

DAVID. You see Elizabeth, I have come to ask your hand in marriage.

ELIZABETH. How dare you make such a proposal?! Your brother has barely been in the ground a month.

JOHN. I know that this all seems sudden, but I think that this is a very good idea.

DAVID. You see Elizabeth, I've been in love with you for a very long time, but I couldn't express my feelings because you were married to my brother. Now that he's gone I thought that I should make my feelings known.

ELIZABETH. It was your idea for me to go to New York, John. Have you changed your mind?

JOHN. I think it's best for your son that he grow up with someone who can be a real father to him.

ELIZABETH. You could be a father to him!

JOHN. It wouldn't be the same. I have obligations of my own. Besides you're a young woman. Surely you don't plan to stay single forever. If you marry a man who has no relation to your son, how will your son be treated? Stepparents are notoriously cruel to their stepchildren. If you marry David you know that he will love Isaiah Junior as his father would have.

ELIZABETH. You make excellent points John. And I wouldn't be averse to marrying David except for the fact that he's an abolitionist! Do you know that he had the audacity to tell me to free my slaves!

DAVID. John and I have had several conversations regarding this matter. If you agree to marry me, then I won't object to you keeping the slaves.

ELIZABETH. Not objecting will not be enough. If we marry you will be master of this plantation. And as master you must not show these niggers one ounce of kindness. Kindness ruins those animals.

DAVID. I understand. Your beauty is the light of my life. I am willing to do anything to secure your love.

JOHN. So are we agreed? Will you marry David?

ELIZABETH. I will.

JOHN. Excellent! I'll perform the ceremony this evening.

Scene Six

*(At rise, **DAVID**, **JOHN**, and **ELIZABETH** are finishing breakfast. They are fairly drunk. They like to drink mint juleps during breakfast before they have morning mass and say their prayers.)*

JOHN. I'm glad that you've seen the light David! Abolition is the worst thing for these niggers! And I know firsthand. Abolishing slavery in New York in 1827 ruined every last one of them. They have no idea what to do with themselves! They drink all day and look for white women to rape at night. New York has become the devil's playground. I think that I might come to live down here in Virginia permanently. I feel that god's great spirit permeates this land.

DAVID. Benjamin! Charlotte! Come clean these dishes and get ready for morning mass.

> *(**BENJAMIN** and **CHARLOTTE** enter and start cleaning the dishes.)*

ELIZABETH. *(Goes to pour herself another mint julep, but the jug is empty.)* My lord! It looks like we'll have to make another jug of mint julep before morning mass.

DAVID. Excuse me.

> *(He gets up and grabs **CHARLOTTE**'s butt as he exits.)*

JOHN. Mass will begin in ten minutes.

> *(He exits.)*

BENJAMIN. Do you want me to finish making that julep for you missus?

ELIZABETH. Thank you Benjamin.

> *(She exits.)*

> *(**BENJAMIN** finishes making the mint julep, then he and **CHARLOTTE** pass the jug back and forth, drinking deeply.)*

CHARLOTTE. *(Laughing.)* We're gonna have to mix some more or else they'll notice.

> **(BENJAMIN** *makes another batch of mint julep in the same jug and then exits.)*

Scene Seven

(CHARLOTTE and BENJAMIN enter mass in the parlor of the house. When BENJAMIN enters, he fills JOHN, DAVID, and ELIZABETH's glasses with the mint julep. He then sits down in a chair and puts the jar down on the table next to him.)

JOHN. *(Reads from Psalm 88.)* I call to you, O Lord, every day;

I spread out my hands to you.

Do you show your wonders to the dead?

Do those who are dead rise up and praise you?

Is your love declared in the grave,

Your faithfulness in Destruction?

Are your wonders known in the place of darkness,

Or your righteous deed in the land of oblivion?

But I cry to you for help, O Lord;

In the morning my prayer comes before you.

Why, O Lord, do you reject me and hide your face from me?

From my youth I have been afflicted and close to death;

I have suffered your terrors and am in despair.

Your wrath has swept over me;

Your terrors have destroyed me.

All day long they surround me like a flood;

They have completely engulfed me.

You have taken my companions

And loved ones from me;

The darkness is my closest friend.

Amen.

ALL. Amen.

JOHN. Let us bow our heads, and pray for our dear departed brother Isaiah. Let us pray in silence.

(They all bow their heads, except **BENJAMIN**. *He takes the jug of mint julep and starts to drink it. It is spilling out the sides of his mouth. He goes to put the jug back and accidentally knocks it onto the floor. Everyone looks up.)*

DAVID. What on earth Benjamin?!

BENJAMIN. I'm – I'm – sorry massa.

JOHN. See David! This is what comes from being kind to niggers! They think they can drink your mint julep and rape your women! Now there's only one way to reprimand this nigger. You must resort to the lash.

BENJAMIN. No massa please.

JOHN. Have you ever been whipped before?

BENJAMIN. No reverend, Massa Isaiah was very kind.

DAVID. That's going to change today Benjamin.

ELIZABETH. Is this really necessary?

JOHN. Don't let your wife meddle in men's affairs.

DAVID. You're the one who told me that I couldn't show an ounce of kindness.

ELIZABETH. *(Pleading.)* Yes David, I did, but this is Benjamin. David, you grew up with him.

DAVID. Stay out of this woman. John, tie Benjamin up to the whipping post.

*(**JOHN** starts to drag **BENJAMIN** out.)*

BENJAMIN. No massa! Please! Please! I won't do it no more!

JOHN. Stop that infernal racket! He that converteth a sinner from the error of his ways shall save his soul from death.

DAVID. He's right Benjamin. This is god's will.

*(**JOHN** continues to drag **BENJAMIN**, and **DAVID** follows. **JOHN** ties **BENJAMIN** to the whipping post, then whips him three times to show **DAVID** how it's done. **JOHN** holds out the whip for **DAVID** to take. He reluctantly takes the whip*

and gets into position to whip **BENJAMIN**. *He can't do it. He hesitates.)*

JOHN. Remember David, this is God's will.

*(***DAVID*** looks at ***ELIZABETH***, and she nods solemnly.)*

*(***DAVID*** then whips ***BENJAMIN*** seven times. Each time, ***BENJAMIN*** let's out an excruciating scream.)*

Scene Eight

> *(At rise, **DAVID** is alone in his study, writing.*
> ***CHARLOTTE** enters.)*

CHARLOTTE. You wanted to see me massa?

DAVID. Yes. How's Isaiah Junior doing?

CHARLOTTE. His fever is still very high.

DAVID. Have you been bathing him with a cold washcloth?

CHARLOTTE. Yes sir. Every quarter of an hour.

DAVID. Send Benjamin for the doctor and then come back straight away.

> *(**CHARLOTTE** leaves for a couple of moments,*
> *then re-enters.)*

CHARLOTTE. Where's mistress?

DAVID. She and John are playing croquet with some of the neighbors.

CHARLOTTE. Do she know how sick little Isaiah is?

DAVID. She needed to take her mind off things for a while.

> *(Pause.)*

Shut the door Charlotte.

> *(**CHARLOTTE** shuts the door.)*

Do you love Benjamin?

CHARLOTTE. With all my heart!

DAVID. Many people believe that niggers don't have feelings, but I believe that they do.

CHARLOTTE. Yes master.

DAVID. Would you like to be free?

CHARLOTTE. Well master. That's a tough question. You know that I love it here with you, mistress, and Reverend John. And you take such good care of us. I honestly can't imagine a situation where I would be happier.
But yes, part of me does wonder what it would be like to be free.

DAVID. I'd like to make you an offer. I'm willing to let you and Benjamin buy your freedom in exchange for some kindness and caring on your part.

CHARLOTTE. What do you mean?

DAVID. I mean Charlotte, that you are one of the most exquisite creatures that I've ever set eyes upon. Ever since I came back, I've thought about you day and night. Charlotte, if the law permitted I would marry you. I need you.

(He grabs her and kisses her deeply.)

CHARLOTTE. Are you sure the mistress would agree to let us buy our freedom?

DAVID. Don't worry about the mistress. I'm the master of this house.

*(The baby starts crying. **DAVID** and **CHARLOTTE** kiss again. He bends her over his desk, pulls up her skirt, and has sex with her very quickly. He should finish after about ten pumps. He pulls out, buttons up, and regains his composure.)*

The baby's crying. Go tend to your duties.

CHARLOTTE. Yes master.

(She straightens up and exits.)

Scene Nine

*(At rise, **DAVID**, **JOHN**, **BENJAMIN**, **ELIZABETH**, **CHARLOTTE**, and the **DOCTOR** are surrounding the baby. The **DOCTOR** holds a stethoscope to the baby's heart.)*

DOCTOR. He's gone to heaven. I'm sorry.

ELIZABETH. *(Starts crying.)* No. No. My baby.
*(Screaming at **CHARLOTTE**.)* This is all your fault! This is all your fault! You killed her!

> *(She starts hitting **CHARLOTTE**. **CHARLOTTE** tries to protect her head and face. **JOHN** pulls out a bible and recites Psalm 23. Sometime during the prayer, **ELIZABETH** grows tired of beating **CHARLOTTE** and stops.)*

JOHN. The lord is my Shepherd, I shall lack nothing.
He makes me lie down in green pastures,
He leads me beside quiet waters,
He restores my soul.
He guides me in paths of righteousness
For his name's sake.
Even though I walk
Through the valley of the shadow
Of death,
I will fear no evil,
For you are with me;
Your rod and your staff,
They comfort me.
You prepare a table before me
In the presence of my enemies.
You anoint my head with oil;
My cup overflows.
Surely goodness and love will follow me
All the days of my life,

And I will dwell in the house of
the lord
forever.
Amen.

ALL. Amen.

Scene Ten

*(At rise, **ELIZABETH** and **DAVID** are alone. He is comforting her.)*

DAVID. Everything's going to be all right Beth. We can not stand in the way of god's will.

ELIZABETH. I know. But it upsets me that Isaiah doesn't have an heir to carry on his name. He was such a good man. Our baby was so beautiful.

DAVID. We could have a baby of our very own.

ELIZABETH. *(With a smile.)* I'm already pregnant.

DAVID. Really?! Are you sure?

ELIZABETH. Absolutely. I was going to wait and surprise you.

DAVID. This is wonderful. I've always wanted to be a father! *(Rubs her stomach, starts speaking to the baby.)* Can you hear me? This is your daddy speaking. Daddy and Mommy are going to take good care of you.

I love you Beth.

ELIZABETH. I love you too.

(Pause.)

I think we should sell Charlotte.

DAVID. Why?

ELIZABETH. I can't bear to look at her face after what she did to little Isaiah.

DAVID. She's a good servant Elizabeth. I don't think that she had anything to do with Isaiah Junior's death. God works in mysterious ways.

ELIZABETH. Charlotte was the one who nursed Isaiah. I know that she neglected him in some way.

DAVID. What about Benjamin?

ELIZABETH. Benjamin can marry one of our other slaves.

DAVID. *(Hesitant.)* How – how about we allow Charlotte and Benjamin to buy their freedom.

ELIZABETH. *(In disbelief.)* Are you listening to me David? My baby is dead because of Charlotte and you suggest that we allow her to buy her freedom?! If you ever speak to me about freeing another one of our slaves, I'll see to it that my brother advocates for our divorce. *(Screams.)* She killed my baby and I want her sold!

DAVID. All right Elizabeth. All right.

I'm sorry.

I'll talk to the trader abut selling Charlotte tomorrow.

Scene Eleven

*(At rise, **BENJAMIN** and **ELIZABETH** are having sex. She is on top. She has an orgasm. She regains her composure and climbs off of him. She straightens herself, fixes her hair, etc.)*

ELIZABETH. I'm going to town for a couple of hours. Take care of the house while I'm gone.

BENJAMIN. Yes ma'am.

*(He straightens himself and climbs out of the bed. **ELIZABETH** exits.)*

*(**BENJAMIN** then goes to the closet and takes out some of Isaiah's clothes and puts them on. He then pretends that he's a slave master.)*

(Pointing.) Nigger! I'm going to take my supper outside this evening. I want you to stand by my table and swat away the flies.

VOICE OF IMAGINARY SLAVE. Yes master.

*(**BENJAMIN** sits and pretends to eat.)*

BENJAMIN. That's not how you swat flies nigger! You're swatting too fast! Swat in a circular motion like this.

(He demonstrates how to swat flies properly.)

VOICE OF IMAGINARY SLAVE. I'm sorry master. Thanks for showing me how to swat flies properly.

BENJAMIN. You're lucky I'm such a good master or I would've had you whupped.

VOICE OF IMAGINARY SLAVE. Thank you kind master.

BENJAMIN. This food's too cold. Go fetch me another plate.

*(He gets up. The **IMAGINARY SLAVE** exits in his mind. A few moments later, the **IMAGINARY SLAVE** runs onstage, running in circles, chased by **DAVID** and **JOHN**.)*

IMAGINARY SLAVE. I didn't steal the meat! I didn't steal the meat!

DAVID. We know you stole it.

JOHN. Give it back.

IMAGINARY SLAVE. I didn't steal the meat! I didn't steal the meat!

BENJAMIN. It's a mortal sin to lie to a white man nigger! We know that you stole the meat. But I know that that's not all you've stolen. I saw you steal a watermelon from the melon patch yesterday evening.

IMAGINARY SLAVE. I swear that I ain't stolen no watermelon either.

BENJAMIN. *(Breaks into song. The singing should be operatic.*)*
VILE NIGGER!

JOHN & DAVID.
YOU'RE A VILE VILE NIGGER.

BENJAMIN.
VILE NIGGER!

JOHN & DAVID.
YOU'RE A VILE VILE NIGGER.

> *(They sing the words "vile vile nigger" in a three-part harmony while they tie a noose around the* **IMAGINARY SLAVE**'s *neck and lynch him. After the* **IMAGINARY SLAVE** *is dead, they sing in unison.)*

BENJAMIN, JOHN & DAVID.
"HE THAT CONVERTETH A SINNER FROM THE ERROR OF HIS WAYS SHALL SAVE A SOUL FROM DEATH."

> *(At this point,* **BENJAMIN**'s *fantasy ends. He can hear* **CHARLOTTE** *calling him.)*

CHARLOTTE. *(Offstage.)* Benjamin. Benjamin? Is you up there?

BENJAMIN. Yes Charlotte. I'll be right down.

> *(He quickly changes out of Isaiah's clothes and puts his own back on.)*

---

*A license to produce *Southern Promises* does not include a performance license for any third-party or copyrighted melodies. Licensees should create their own.

Scene Twelve

(*At rise,* **BENJAMIN** *and* **CHARLOTTE** *are eating dinner.*)

BENJAMIN. You sure do know how to cook up some pig's feet and collard greens. I swear your cookin' is better than my mama's.

CHARLOTTE. Thank you Benjamin.

BENJAMIN. I've got to go back out tonight. Master John needs me to chop up some firewood and bring it into the house.

CHARLOTTE. I have to tell you something. But I'm hesitant to say anything because of all the lies we've been told.

BENJAMIN. What?

CHARLOTTE. Master David told me that he would allow us to buy our freedom.

BENJAMIN. Really? How did this come up?

CHARLOTTE. Master David just brought me into his study and asked me whether we wanted our freedom.

BENJAMIN. What did you have to do for him?

(*Pause.* **CHARLOTTE** *doesn't answer.*)

What did you have to do for him?

(*Pause. She still doesn't answer.* **BENJAMIN** *violently grabs her hair.*)

What did you have to do for him you slut?!

CHARLOTTE. Nothing! I ain't do nothing for him.

BENJAMIN. You lie!

(*He is about to hit her when* **DAVID** *walks in.*)

DAVID. What's going on here?

(**BENJAMIN** *releases* **CHARLOTTE**'s *hair.*)

Benjamin, it is a sin to raise your hand against your wife. You must fight your animal instincts and try to be civilized. Now apologize to Charlotte.

(*Pause.*)

BENJAMIN. I'm sorry Charlotte.

CHARLOTTE. I'm sorry too.

DAVID. Good.

Charlotte, gather your things.

CHARLOTTE. Why, Master David?

DAVID. Don't ask questions Charlotte. Just gather your things.

BENJAMIN. Where you taking her master?

DAVID. Didn't John tell you to chop some firewood? It's freezing in the house.

BENJAMIN. Can't I finish my supper?

DAVID. No you can not finish your supper. If you ever question me again I'm going to whip you twice as severely as I whipped you before. Now chop that wood nigger!

BENJAMIN. Yes master.

> (**CHARLOTTE** and **BENJAMIN** just stare at each other for a moment. They are uncertain whether they will ever see each other again.)

Bye Charlotte.

> (He goes over and kisses her.)

CHARLOTTE. Bye Benjamin. I love you.

DAVID. Stop this nonsense!

> (He pushes **BENJAMIN** out the door.)

BENJAMIN. (Frantic.) I love you too! I love you Charlotte. I love you.

DAVID. Don't say another word! Just get that wood!

CHARLOTTE. Where are you taking me?

DAVID. Never mind that. Gather up your things. Your train leaves soon.

CHARLOTTE. Am I being sold?

DAVID. (Overwhelmed with desire.) I need to have you one last time. I'm going to miss this.

> (He violently lifts up her skirt and shoves himself into her.)

DAVID. *(Panting.)* I'm going to miss this!
I'm going to miss this!
Sweet nigger pussy!
I love you. I love you.

(He pulls himself out of her.)

Let's go.

(They start to leave, but then he speaks.)

Remember, the lord giveth and the lord taketh away.

(He tries to stop himself from kissing her on the lips, but he can't help himself and kisses her anyway.)

Scene Thirteen

*(At rise, **BENJAMIN** is lying despondently in bed. **DAVID** is sitting in **BENJAMIN**'s bed, rubbing his arm, and **ELIZABETH** is in a chair next to him. **JOHN** brings in a turkey leg and cornbread on a plate. He is eating cornbread.)*

DAVID. We've let you lie here for two days because of your grief, but now it's time to move on Benjamin.

ELIZABETH. We know how much you loved Charlotte, but we think that you should take a new wife to console yourself. Are there any of our slave girls that you would like to marry? I've always noticed that you like Frieda.

BENJAMIN. I don't want a new wife. I love Charlotte.

JOHN. God works in mysterious ways Benjamin. You must toss off your grief and take a new wife.

ELIZABETH. We've brought you a turkey leg and some cornbread to make you feel better.

BENJAMIN. You brung me a turkey leg?

DAVID. Yes. We know it's your favorite.

*(**JOHN** hands **DAVID** the plate of food, and **BENJAMIN** eats ferociously.)*

ELIZABETH. Is there any slave girl on another plantation that you like?

BENJAMIN. I don't want another wife. Even though she's been taken away we're still bound by god.

DAVID. Suit yourself Benjamin, but you must return to work tomorrow.

BENJAMIN. Yes master.

ELIZABETH. We're so glad to see that you're feeling better. Remember that we're here to comfort you.

JOHN. We expect to see you at morning mass tomorrow. You can even have a mint julep.

BENJAMIN. Thank you Master John.

*(**JOHN** pats **BENJAMIN** on the back.)*

ELIZABETH. Good night Benjamin.

DAVID. Good night.

BENJAMIN. Good night.

(They exit, and **BENJAMIN** *is left alone.)*

Scene Fourteen

(It is eight months later. **ELIZABETH** *is in labor.* **JOHN**, **DAVID**, *and the* **DOCTOR** *are standing around the bed.* **ELIZABETH** *is screaming.)*

DOCTOR. Push. Push. You're almost there Elizabeth.

ELIZABETH. I'm pushing!

DAVID. Just keep it up! You're doing a great job dear.

DOCTOR. Here it comes!

*(***ELIZABETH** *gives one final push and scream and we hear the baby crying. The baby is black.)*

You have a beautiful baby girl Elizabeth.

(The **DOCTOR** *hands the baby to* **DAVID**. **DAVID** *and* **JOHN** *are horrified that the baby's black but try to keep their composure.)*

ELIZABETH. I want to hold the baby. I want to see her.

DAVID. Not right now Elizabeth. You should rest.

JOHN. Yes. Yes. You should rest.

ELIZABETH. Just hand her to me for a moment.

DOCTOR. They're right Elizabeth. You should sleep.

Scene Fifteen

(It is later that night. **JOHN** *and* **DAVID** *are alone.)*

DAVID. Are you sure that there's no nigger blood in your family.

JOHN. Absolutely. Don't insult my ancestors!

DAVID. I'm sorry. But that baby is a nigger child. That means that that slut has had relations with some nigger.

JOHN. Elizabeth is a virtuous and righteous woman. There must be some other explanation.

DAVID. Like what?

JOHN. Maybe there's some nigger blood in your family.

*(***DAVID*** *slaps* ***JOHN.****)*

DAVID. Don't ever insult my heritage!

JOHN. Maybe she was raped.

DAVID. That slut wasn't raped! She would've had that nigger hung if she had been. She's done the unthinkable.

JOHN. You're right. My fair sister has compromised her chastity. What are we going to do?

DAVID. Kill the child.

JOHN. Can't we –

DAVID. We must kill the child. If we kill it now then people will believe that the child was weak and didn't survive the night. It happens all the time.

JOHN. You're right. We must not let shame be cast upon this family.

DAVID. Will you go get it?

JOHN. Yes.

(He exits and then comes back with the baby in a blanket.)

How should we do it?

(The baby starts crying.)

DAVID. Here. Let me.

> *(*JOHN *hands the baby to* DAVID.*)*

> *(*DAVID *lays the baby down on a table and strangles it. We hear gasping sounds. Then all is silent.)*

Poor, poor, innocent thing. Brought into this world through sin.

JOHN. Let us pray for the innocent nigger child.

> *(He and* DAVID *recite traditional funeral prayers.)*

JOHN.

Heavenly Father,

you have not made us for darkness and death,

but for life with you for ever.

Without you we have nothing to hope for;

with you we have nothing to fear.

Speak to us now your words of eternal life.

Lift us from anxiety and guilt

to the light and peace of your presence,

and set the glory of your love before us;

through Jesus Christ our Lord.

DAVID. Lord Jesus Christ,

you comforted your disciples when you were going to die:

now set our troubled hearts at rest

and banish our fears.

You are the way to the Father:

help us to follow you.

You are the truth:

bring us to know you.

You are the life:

give us that life,

to live with you now and for ever.

JOHN. O God, who brought us to birth,

and in whose arms we die,

in our grief and shock

contain and comfort us;
embrace us with your love,
give us hope in our confusion
and grace to let go into new life;
through Jesus Christ.
Amen.

DAVID. Amen.

      (Pause.)

Let's bury the child in the backyard. We'll bury it by the stream at the edge of the plantation. No one will find it there.

JOHN. Wrap the child in blankets. I'll go get a shovel.

      *(**DAVID** starts to wrap the baby, and **JOHN** exits.)*

Scene Sixteen

*(At rise, **BENJAMIN** is in his bed, sleeping. The ghost of his old master, **ISAIAH**, walks into the room and wakes him. Maybe **BENJAMIN** is dreaming. Maybe he isn't. **ISAIAH**'s voice should sound majestic.)*

ISAIAH. Benjamin! Rise from your slumber!

BENJAMIN. *(Wakes up, startled. Scared.)* What?! Who's there?!

ISAIAH. *(Moves closer to him.)* It's me Benjamin. Your master Isaiah.

BENJAMIN. But you's dead master. You's must be a ghost.

ISAIAH. We never die Benjamin. We just take on a different form. Don't be afraid.

BENJAMIN. What do you want with me?

ISAIAH. You are in grave danger. You must leave this place.

BENJAMIN. Why am I in danger?

ISAIAH. I think you know why Benjamin. Something having to do with a child.

BENJAMIN. Forgive me master. I didn't want to do it. I'm sorry.

ISAIAH. All is forgiven. God forgives. But you must leave this place tomorrow.

BENJAMIN. Where should I go?

ISAIAH. Go north. Go to that freedom which I promised you. You'll be safe there.

BENJAMIN. Can I take Charlotte?

ISAIAH. Charlotte's gone Benjamin. She's gone. You will be reunited with her in heaven.

BENJAMIN. How can I escape?

ISAIAH. Use your two feet.

BENJAMIN. That's not what I mean master. Where should I go? How do I not get caught?

ISAIAH. *(Starts to exit.)* Your heart will guide you. The lord speaks to you through your heart.

BENJAMIN. That's it? That's all you gonna tell me?

(There is no answer.)

Master? Master?

*(**ISAIAH** is gone. **BENJAMIN** gets out of bed and puts his clothes on. He leaves his room.)*

Scene Seventeen

*(At rise, **JOHN** and **DAVID** are walking back from burying the baby. They are covered in dirt.)*

JOHN. Are you sure that it's Benjamin?

DAVID. Who else could it be? He's the only male house nigger.

JOHN. What should we do with him?

DAVID. We should act normal all day tomorrow, so that he doesn't suspect anything. And tomorrow night we should knock him unconscious while he's sleeping, castrate him, then bury him alive.

JOHN. That'll teach the nigger never to touch a white woman.

DAVID. That *will* teach the nigger.

Scene Eighteen

*(At rise, **DAVID** enters **ELIZABETH**'s room. She is very sick from childbirth. She looks pale and weak.)*

DAVID. How are you feeling Beth?

ELIZABETH. I feel very weak.

DAVID. Is there anything that I can get you?

ELIZABETH. A glass of water would help.

*(**DAVID** goes and gets a glass of water, then returns. He holds the glass of water just out of her reach so that she has to struggle to take the glass from his hand.)*

DAVID. Do you feel better now?

ELIZABETH. Yes.

*(**DAVID** sits in a chair near the bed.)*

DAVID. Have you seen Benjamin today?

ELIZABETH. No. I called for him a couple of times but he never came.

DAVID. Neither have I. I've had the whole plantation searched and there's no sign of him.

ELIZABETH. *(Alarmed.)* It's almost evening. Why didn't you tell me earlier?

DAVID. I didn't want to alarm you.

ELIZABETH. When was the last time anyone saw him?

DAVID. Last night.

ELIZABETH. That's not like Benjamin. Where do you think he is?

DAVID. I think he escaped.

ELIZABETH. Benjamin loves us. Why would he escape?

DAVID. I think you would know better than I.

ELIZABETH. What's that supposed to mean?

DAVID. Exactly what it sounds like. I think that you would know better than I.

ELIZABETH. I want to see my baby. Can I see my baby now?

DAVID. No. *Your* baby caused this whole mess.

ELIZABETH. David. You're scaring me.

DAVID. *(Gets up and goes over to the bed.)* What reason do you have to be scared? You've done nothing wrong.

ELIZABETH. I – I haven't done anything.

> *(**DAVID** slowly grabs a pillow.)*

DAVID. *(Leans into her and speaks in a sinister tone.)* I know what you did. You've dishonored this family.

ELIZABETH. I didn't do anything!

DAVID. *(Slaps her across the face really hard.)* You're a damned liar. This is god's punishment for having relations with a nigger you damned slut!

> *(He violently puts the pillow over her face and smothers her. Her legs kick and there is a struggle. Eventually she stops moving. He removes the pillow from her face.)*
>
> *(He is quiet for a few moments. Then he runs to the door, shouting for John.)*

John! John! Where are you?

> *(He runs out of the room to look for John.)*

(Offstage.) John! John! Come here.

JOHN. *(Offstage.)* What? What's going on.

DAVID. *(Offstage.)* Something terrible has happened.

> *(They enter.)*

I came to check on her and she was dead.

JOHN. Oh my dear sister.

> *(He goes over to **ELIZABETH** and holds her hand and kisses her forehead.)*

My dear dear sister.

> *(He cries.)*

God has punished her for her wickedness.

DAVID. I fear he has.

JOHN. Let us pray for her soul.

(He recites Psalm 90.)

Lord, you have been our refuge
Throughout all generations.
Before the mountains were born or you brought forth
the earth
And the world,
From everlasting to everlasting
You are god.
You turn men back to dust,
Saying, "Return to dust, O sons of men."
For a thousand years in your sight
Are like a day that has just gone by,
Or like the new grass of the morning –
Though in the morning it springs up new,
By evening it is dry and withered.
We are consumed by your anger and terrified by your
indignation.
You have set our iniquities before you,
Our secret sins in the light of your presence.
All our days pass away under your wrath;
We finish our years with a moan.
The length of our days is seventy years –
Or eighty, if we have the strength;
Yet their span is but trouble and sorrow,
For they quickly pass, and we fly away.
Oh lord please deliver Elizabeth's soul to heaven and
pardon her sins.
In Christ's name.
Amen.

DAVID. Amen.

(Pause.)

I'm going to free all the slaves on this plantation John.

JOHN. You should think about this for a couple of days, David. Think about all the money you could get if you sold them.

DAVID. Those slaves are *my* property and I will free them. This is god's will. Now run and tell the overseer to stop all work on this plantation, and let it be known that from this moment all my slaves are free.

JOHN. *(Thinks about arguing some more, but sees that it's of no use.)* I'll tell the overseer.

> *(He runs out of the room.)*

DAVID. *(Opens the window and starts shouting out.)* You're free! You're free! Do you hear?

> *(He runs offstage, and we can hear him shouting.)*

(Offstage.) You're free! You're free! You're free!

Scene Nineteen

(Three years later. At rise, **BENJAMIN** *is in a small shop working at a table, fixing a shoe. A white man,* **ATTICUS BUFORD**, *enters.)*

ATTICUS. Good morning Mr. Freeman!

BENJAMIN. Good morning Mr. Buford.

ATTICUS. You got something for me?

BENJAMIN. *(Laughs.)* When have I ever paid my rent late?

(He opens a drawer and hands **ATTICUS** *a wad of cash.)*

ATTICUS. You are mighty right about that Mr. Freeman. You always have the money on the exact day the rent is due. And I appreciate that. Some of these white folks keep me waiting for days. Sometimes, I even have to take them to court! But not you Mr. Freeman. I'll tell you the truth. I didn't want to rent this shop to you. When you came to me three years ago, I thought that you had been sent by your master, but then you explained that you had been manumitted, and wanted to rent the shop for yourself, and my jaw nearly hit the floor. I thought to myself: "This is one uppity nigger, thinkin' that he gonna run his own store." You see, I was afraid that my niggers might get it in their head that they should be free too.

BENJAMIN. So, why did you rent it to me?

ATTICUS. This shop had been empty for six months, and I needed the money. But I'm glad that I rented it to you. You've shown all the white folks around here what a good nigger can be. A nigger like you must have some white blood 'cause –

BENJAMIN. Could you please stop referring to me as a nigger?

ATTICUS. Yes, Mr. Freeman, I'm sorry. We all know that you prefer not to be called a nigger. I got a little carried away is all. How's Mrs. Freeman?

BENJAMIN. *(A huge grin comes across his face.)* Charlotte's pregnant!

ATTICUS. Congratulations! I remember when I had my first child. Happiest time of my life.

BENJAMIN. Is that Ruth? Was she your first?

ATTICUS. *(Quietly.)* No, my first was a beautiful boy we called Samuel. Died at the age of four.

> *(Wipes his eye.)*

But such is life. The important thing is to savor each moment you have with your children, for no day is guaranteed.

> *(**BENJAMIN** doesn't know what to say to this. He looks at **ATTICUS** with deep empathy.)*

Well, I best be going. More rent to collect! Goodbye Mr. Freeman.

BENJAMIN. Goodbye Mr. Buford.

Scene Twenty

*(At home that evening, **CHARLOTTE** sits alone in their dining room, knitting. **BENJAMIN** enters and gives her a kiss.)*

BENJAMIN. How are you feeling?

CHARLOTTE. I think I felt him kick today.

BENJAMIN. You did?

(He goes over and feels her belly.)

I think I feel something.

CHARLOTTE. I'm pretty sure that's his elbow.

(Pause.)

(They smile at each other.)

BENJAMIN. Is dinner ready?

CHARLOTTE. *(Calling to the kitchen.)* Sarah?

SARAH. *(Offstage.)* Yes.

CHARLOTTE. How long until dinner's ready?

SARAH. *(Offstage.)* It's ready. I was just waiting for master to get home.

CHARLOTTE. Master's here.

SARAH. *(Offstage.)* I didn't hear him come in!

CHARLOTTE. *(To **BENJAMIN**.)* Is she deaf? How can she say she didn't hear you come in? It's not like we live in a mansion?

*(**SARAH** enters with another slave, **EMMANUEL**, and they serve **BENJAMIN** and **CHARLOTTE**.)*

CHARLOTTE. Did you talk to Mr. Buford about buying the shop?

BENJAMIN. Not today. I couldn't find the right moment.

CHARLOTTE. There's never going to be a "right" moment. You just have to ask him. No, no, you're going to tell him! "Mr. Buford, I've decided to purchase this shop. How much do you want for it?"

*(**BENJAMIN** laughs. **CHARLOTTE** laughs too.)*

BENJAMIN. *(Excitedly.)* That's good, that's good! How about: "Mr. Buford, I'm going to buy this shop, and I've decided to give you seven hundred and fifty dollars for it."

> *(They laugh some more.)*

CHARLOTTE. I think it might actually work!

> *(There is a loud knock on the door.)*

You expecting someone?

BENJAMIN. No.

SARAH. Master, do you want me to answer that?

BENJAMIN. *(Condescendingly.)* Yes, Sarah.

> **(SARAH** *answers the door.)*

SARAH. May I help you?

DAVID. Yes, I'm looking for Mr. Benjamin Freeman. Does he live here?

BENJAMIN. *(To* **CHARLOTTE.***)* Go hide.

> **(CHARLOTTE** *gets up from the table and exits.* **BENJAMIN** *goes to the door and confronts* **DAVID. SARAH** *stands aside.)*

What do you want?

DAVID. Is this your new wife, Benjamin?

> *(He looks* **SARAH** *up and down lasciviously.)*

If so, you did very well for yourself. I dare say she's more beautiful than Charlotte.

BENJAMIN. What do you want?

DAVID. I've come to reclaim my property!

> *(He pushes past* **BENJAMIN** *and goes into the house. He takes a seat.)*

BENJAMIN. I don't want any trouble.

DAVID. Then you and your new wife need to pack your bags and come with me.

BENJAMIN. I'm not your property anymore.

DAVID. Yes, you are. And to add insult to injury you changed your last name to "Freeman" which is the biggest lie I ever heard!

BENJAMIN. You freed all your slaves. The day after I left. That means I'm free too.

DAVID. I did not free all my slaves. I had manumission papers drawn up for every slave that was on my property that day. So all of my slaves were freed, except one. Do you know what I've been through to find you? I've had slave catchers on the hunt for you, searching in every northern state. For a while, I lost all hope, thinking that you'd escaped to Canada. You outsmarted me, I'll give you that. I assumed that you'd go north. I thought, "What nigger would have the nerve to stay in the south after he's run away?" So you had me looking in all the wrong places, but at last I've found you.

BENJAMIN. Why are you doing this?

DAVID. Because you fucked my wife Benjamin – made me look like a damn fool! I killed that black baby so that no one would find out, but the damn doctor blabbed his mouth all around town. Everywhere I went I heard people whispering cuckold. Cuckold. There's the man who couldn't satisfy his own wife, so she went and fucked a nigger! Do you know how embarrassing that was?! My family name is ruined.

BENJAMIN. Leave!

DAVID. *(Pulls out a gun.)* You're coming with me!

> *(**BENJAMIN** grabs **DAVID**'s arm to avoid being shot. They struggle. The gun fires, but no one is hurt. **BENJAMIN** is eventually able to knock the gun out of **DAVID**'s hand. **BENJAMIN** and **DAVID** continue to fight. It is brutal. **CHARLOTTE** enters the room, picks up the gun, and shoots **DAVID** in the head. The struggle ends.)*

CHARLOTTE. Is he dead?

> *(**BENJAMIN** nods his head.)*

Sarah, where's Emmanuel?

SARAH. I don't know.

> *(**EMMANUEL** sheepishly enters from another room.)*

BENJAMIN. Your master gets attacked, so you run and hide?!

> *(He grabs his whip and approaches* **EMMANUEL.** **CHARLOTTE** *grabs* **BENJAMIN.***)*

CHARLOTTE. No Benjamin! They have to dispose of David's body right now. You can whip him later.

BENJAMIN. You're right.

> *(To* **SARAH** *and* **EMMANUEL.***)* Dig a hole. Bury this pathetic white man out back.

> *(***SARAH** *and* **EMMANUEL** *exit.*)*

CHARLOTTE. Is what he said true? About the black baby?

BENJAMIN. *(Nods his head. Starts to cry.)* I'm sorry Charlotte. She made me. She made me. I hated touching her.

CHARLOTTE. *(Wraps her arms around him.)* I know. I know what it's like. I believe you.

> *(They hold each other for a while, and cry.)*

> *(***CHARLOTTE** *looks at* **DAVID**'*s bloody body.*)*

But now we're finally free.

> *(***BENJAMIN** *looks at* **DAVID**'*s body.*)*

BENJAMIN. Now we're finally free.

> *(They look into each other's eyes and kiss.)*

End of Play